Marie Antoinette AKAMESSE

Customs and the digitization of procedures

Marie Antoinette AKAMESSE

Customs and the digitization of procedures

The contribution of the digitization of customs procedures and the performance of Chad's customs administration

ScienciaScripts

Imprint

Cover image: www.ingimage.com

This book is a translation from the original published under ISBN 978-620-8-82554-6.

Publisher:
Sciencia Scripts
is a trademark of
Dodo Books Indian Ocean Ltd. and OmniScriptum S.R.L publishing group

120 High Road, East Finchley, London, N2 9ED, United Kingdom
Str. Armeneasca 28/1, office 1, Chisinau MD-2012, Republic of Moldova, Europe
Managing Directors: Ieva Konstantinova, Victoria Ursu
info@omniscriptum.com

Printed at: see last page
ISBN: 978-620-3-57327-5

THE CONTRIBUTION OF THE DIGITALISATION OF CUSTOMS PROCEDURES AND THE PERFORMANCE OF THE CUSTOMS ADMINISTRATION IN CHAD

FULL NAME: AKAMESSE MARIE ANTOINETTE

PROFESSION: TEACHER-RESEARCHER

GRADE: ASSISTANT

UNIVERSITY: UNIVERSITY OF EBOLOWA/ CAMEROON /

FACULTY OF LEGAL AND POLITICAL SCIENCES

TEL: +237 699 977 806

E-MAIL : AKAMESSEMARIEANTOINETTE54@GMAIL.COM

SUMMARY

Under the impetus of the World Customs Organisation (WCO) and the World Trade Organisation (WTO), the Chadian customs administration has long included among its strategic choices the use of new information and communication technologies in order to be able to continuously improve the service provided to users and to meet performance requirements. Today, the completion of a number of projects has enabled it to breathe new life into trade facilitation. So, when asked what contribution the digitisation of customs procedures has made to improving the performance of the customs administration in Chad, the answer is twofold. There are two opposing realities. Although the use of automatic customs clearance methods has led to a significant improvement in customs rules for processing trade in Chad, the Chadian customs administration is not sufficiently equipped to meet the challenge posed by the very existence of trade carried out using the new computerised techniques.

Key words: *Digitisation, Customs procedure, Performance, Customs administration*

INTRODUCTION

The evolution of technology[1], is one of the main vectors of economic activity in general in the world, and particularly, it appears nowadays as a factor of development of the modernization of the Customs administrations. The emphasis is on new information and communication technologies and technical tools. Today, the development of new information and communication technologies is essential for customs administrations in general and Chad's in particular. This tool has become essential to customs reforms in the context of globalisation. It is essential to the implementation of the WTO's Trade Facilitation Agreement (TFA)[(2)]. The Larousse dictionary defines trade facilitation as "a set of techniques used to process and transmit information (cable, telephone, Internet, etc.)"[3]. It is therefore in recognition of the importance of this technological tool in facilitating communication and the exchange of information that the WCO has included it in its vision of customs in the 21st century. It is also in this context that Lionel PASCAL recognises that "in the latter part of the 21st century and in the 21st century, technology has enabled major advances in the development of goods"[4].In Chad, the automation of customs procedures is taking place in a climate of harmonisation and standardisation of the legal instruments of the Central African Economic and Monetary Community (CEMAC). This process began a long time ago[5]. Until now, the automation of customs procedures has not been codified, but has been carried out on the basis of the recommendations of the WCO, of which the Chadian Republic is a member. The latter applied the provisions of the revised Kyoto International Convention on the simplification and harmonisation of customs procedures, which states in its preamble that "the adoption of modern techniques such as risk management systems and audit controls, as well as the widest possible use of information technology"[6]. It is with Regulation No. 05/19-UEAC -010 A-CM-33, Portant revision du Code des Douanes de la Communauté Économique et Monétaire de l'Afrique Central (CEMAC) in its Article 66 (1) that Community legislation has sought to be in harmony with recent developments in international customs law. The transposition of this article into the national normative architecture has intersected with the vast IT reform programme for the modernisation of Chadian administrations in order to offer users quality services, launched in November 2020, by "the Ministry of Finance, Budget and Public Accounts (MFBCP), in partnership with the General Directorate of Customs and Indirect Duties. They have officially launched a new automated IT system (ASYCUDA WORLD) to replace ASYCUDA ++"[7]. The aim of this reform is to strengthen the capacity of the Chadian customs administration, to optimise its performance budget and In this way, before any substantive development can take place, it is important to ensure that the country's administrative procedures are in line with international standards in terms of protecting society, securing the supply chain, facilitating trade and supporting businesses. Before delving into the substance of the issue, it is important to understand the very meaning of the concepts of digitisation of customs procedures and performance of the customs administration.

Digitalisation refers to the use of digital technologies and data, as well as the interconnections that give rise to new activities or the development of existing activities[8]. This definition and its translation already make it possible to emphasise that in French the terms "numérique" and "digital" are not perfect synonyms, and to understand why the latter is preferred in this research. It also makes it possible to clearly define the area of interest of this research. The main characteristic of digital is its ability to generate change at a very rapid pace. This means that we have to constantly analyse past developments in order to integrate them, while at the same time trying to make the best possible projections for what will happen next. As a result, the real meaning of these terms is constantly evolving as a function of technological advances and, above all, the way in which organisations appropriate them.

Not to be confused, etymologically digital refers to "number", "calculation" and the conversion of analogue information into binary numbers. So when we talk about digital government, we are mainly referring to the digitisation of work tools, the transition from paper forms to electronic versions, electronic document management (EDM) or contracts, for example. Digital, on the other hand, etymologically refers to the finger. The concept of digitisation encompasses and catalyses a wide range of technologies. Digitisation, computerisation and dematerialisation are all part of this transformation. Digital refers to the new generations who text faster than their thumbs or swipe television screens before they can walk - in short, to those who use their fingers to connect with the world. One wonders what links digital to the customs procedure.

The customs procedure refers to all the operations required on entering or leaving the country in order to collect customs duties. This includes the presentation of goods under the conditions laid down by law, the customs declaration, the verification and settlement of duties by agents and the payment of duties. One author, with a touch of doctrine, defines the customs clearance procedure as "all the formalities that are carried out to assign a customs procedure to the goods, i.e. one of the situations in which they may be placed under customs legislation"[9]. These are the formalities involved in clearing goods for consumption, export, re-export and all suspensive and economic customs procedures. So when we talk about the digitisation of customs procedures, we are referring more broadly to the interweaving of technology in the process. It should be noted that the English word 'digit' is more consensual, referring to both 'number' and 'finger'. There is therefore a lot of talk about digital customs procedures as a fashion statement, but also to emphasise that, beyond the simple technological changes implemented in the customs administration, the digital revolution is profoundly changing all the strategies, processes and practices put in place by the customs administration. The concept of the digitisation of customs procedures can therefore be understood as the interweaving of practices and strategies of the new information and communication technologies by the customs administration and economic operators throughout the customs clearance process. The concept of performance, for its part, is the lever or scale on which this study is based and can be understood in several ways. Performance is an English word meaning "execution, completion; by extension, any achievement"[10]. This definition places the emphasis on what is ultimately sought to be achieved, and corresponds to the definition given by the Organisation for Economic Co-operation and Development (OECD)[11]. Furthermore, the Oxford dictionary offers a definition of performance that focuses more on the means: "the accomplishment, execution, development of whatever has been ordered or undertaken; the execution of any action or work"[12]. According to these definitions, talking about performance means thinking both about the ultimate results we want to achieve and about the appropriate means to achieve them. More concretely, talking about organisational performance means taking an interest in the ultimate results produced by the organisation and the means it uses to produce these results.

Clearly, in traditional public administration, "performance was determined by the assurance of compliance with the laws and regulations in force, the control of resources and the ethics of public service"[13]. This approach was often criticised for being more, or even solely, focused on processes or means rather than results.

What's more, the range of performance criteria used in today's public services has widened, not least because of pressure from the general public and elected representatives. In the The list of the most common performance criteria includes economy[14], effectiveness[15], efficiency, which is similar to the criterion of productivity, the quality of the products or services offered and, finally, budget balance, i.e. the ratio between what was actually spent and the expenditure that had been planned[16].The customs administration, sometimes known as customs, is seen as the official name for the customs service. It is a "government department responsible for the application and control of all measures in force to ensure the enforcement of customs laws and regulations"[17]. The glossary of legal terms defines it as the administrative department responsible for applying customs legislation and collecting import duties and taxes, and which is also responsible for applying other related laws and regulations, including those on the import, transit and export of goods[18]. In general, it is an area of sovereignty, one of the expressions of the transition from a state to a nation. State to another, from one customs post or office to another, where customs checks are carried out just after border police checks[19].The introduction of a performance-based approach[20]in the Chadian customs administration, albeit only recently, would be a welcome development. The government is committed to developing a new administrative culture, one that is more focused on results, and in this case the difficult budgetary and security situation is consubstantial with the new context of digitalisation. Professor PEKASSA NDAM sees these performance indicators as "a benchmark for a scale of measures"[21]. For the Customs Administration, these may be pre-determined objectives, as its agents are no longer judged on compliance with procedures, but on the achievement of objectives. In the same way as other State financial authorities, its achievements are assessed on the basis of "quantitative and qualitative management by objective"[22]. Customs, on the other hand, is on the front line of various changes. Trade liberalisation is increasing its activity and changing its nature: more products, more complex and multimodal logistics, increasingly mobile sourcing, fundamental customs "cash, value, origin, border..."[23], more complex to understand. A fiscal role in which the proportion of customs duties is declining, and crime, which is becoming a massive and intelligent part of trade. In the face of such changes, which are dampening the performance of the customs administration, it is not enough to modernise the law and IT; working methods must also be adapted, new tools developed and staff trained in new professions. In this respect, the question of the contribution of digitising customs procedures to the performance of the Chadian customs administration seems provocative at first sight, given that performance is a current requirement of public management in Chad, without being meaningless. However, digitisation does present a challenge for the Chadian customs administration. While the quest for performance is relatively old for private sector organisations, public sector organisations are paying increasing attention to it.With the performance of the customs administration through digital technology as the subject of this research, the research question can be formulated as follows: **Does the digitisation of customs procedures help to improve the performance of the customs administration in Chad**? The assessment that can be made of the contribution of the digitisation of customs procedures in terms of the performance of the customs administration in Chad is ambivalent. In order to find the answers, we will adopt a methodological approach based essentially on an analysis of Community and Chadian legal texts, without, however, depriving ourselves of a surreptitious look at foreign laws where necessary. Whatever the level of adoption of new information and communication technologies in the customs clearance process in Chad, there is no doubt that digitisation is revolutionising customs procedures, especially traditional customs clearance methods (**I**).Like any business innovation, digitisation "generates revenue but also involves expenditure"[24]and risks that are not conducive to improving the performance of the Chadian customs administration (**II**.).

I. IMPROVED PERFORMANCE THROUGH DIGITISATION OF TRADITIONAL CUSTOMS CLEARANCE METHODS

The automated method of clearing goods, a topical issue in Chad, is a matter for all players in the customs chain, i.e. international, regional and national (public and private) players. There is an African saying that "one hand cannot tie a bundle of wood". The same is true of any large-scale undertaking. The Chad customs administration is no exception to the rule. It is now an axiom, no need to resort to demonstrations. The organic and formal nature of customs law affects all the provisions enabling the State to "control the flow of goods entering or leaving the country". Given its strategic position at the borders, the Customs Administration, in collaboration with other departments[25], implements various laws which have in common the protection of the national or community economy, public health and public finances. In Chad, a vast programme has been launched, resulting in the adoption of laws and regulations establishing and organising the information society. As part of this process, a new CEMAC Customs Code has been adopted, followed by internal texts on the digital world in order to provide a better framework for the digitalisation of customs procedures and formalities for the benefit of the customs administration (**A**) and economic operators (**B**).

A. Substitution of automatic customs clearance methods for traditional methods by the customs administration

The aim of abandoning manual processing of customs documents is to help speed up customs processing and reduce clearance times[26]and certain costs that are sometimes considered unforeseen in customs operations. The aim of this operation is to establish transparency and simplify customs procedures[27]for the benefit of partners. Customs computerisation cannot be limited solely to the actual clearance of goods, but must also extend to transit, which should be tackled at the next stage. Under the impetus of international and regional standards, the Chadian customs administration has adopted reforms that provide a framework for the use of new technologies in traditional customs procedures **(1)**, which are applied primarily to optimise revenue and time **(2)**.

1. Adopting digital reforms to simplify traditional customs procedures

In a context of constant change and globalisation of trade, the Chad Customs Administration, with the support of the public authorities, has embarked on a vast programme of reform and modernisation[28]based on the digitalisation[29]of customs procedures and formalities. Among the modernisation objectives listed by MONTAGNAT- According to RENTIER and PARENT, IT is cited as an "indispensable tool for the success" of all the reforms[30]. This analysis will focus on two digital mechanisms designed to facilitate the exchanges used by Chad's customs administration: the ASYCUDA WORD system (a) and the Scanner (b).

a. **Replacing ASYCUDA ++ with ASYCUDA WORD**

Customs technology has been revolutionised by the way customs services work today, paving the way for greater integration and strengthening the ability of customs administrations to communicate, manage the flow of goods, receive and exchange information, coordinate border activities, cooperate in the fight against fraud and promote transparency[31]. In Chad, the ASYCUDA++ modules have begun to be installed. But the search for performance is motivating the customs service in Chad to migrate to ASYCUDAWORD.

The Sydonia++ computerised customs clearance system has been operational in Chad since 2001[32]. However, ASYCUDA++ will be replaced by ASYCUDAWORD, thanks to the Ministry of Finance and Budget, which is considered to be "an IT system that uses modern technologies and offers full functionality"[33]. This new system "allows tax filers to enter their tax returns from their premises and send them to the tax authorities". electronically with documents attached to the customs office" and "to integrate manifests electronically"[34] Many African countries[35]are now experimenting with computerisation, which describes the application of information and communication technologies (ICTs) to the performance of customs duties. It is a system that makes it possible to handle all customs operations proper, from the moment a declaration is lodged through to the total or partial clearance of goods[36]. The system is being developed in line with the international codes and standards developed by OSI[37], WCO and the United Nations. The ultimate aim of this system is to improve the efficiency of international trade through measures that reform existing procedures and working methods[38]. That said, due to the difficulties encountered by customs officers in implementing computerised customs procedures (ASYCUDA), Single Administrative Documents (SADs) are the main sources of data on international trade in goods. However, as these SADs are filled in manually, errors are often found on these documents, due either to omissions or to a poor understanding of the procedures by the agents responsible for filling them in. The information entered is also frequently crossed out, sometimes making it difficult to read[39]. While in theory the migration from ASYCUDA++ to ASYCUDA WORLD has been launched, the issue of upgrading, which has been raised and strongly supported in the same way as the computerisation of Chadian customs, must be addressed at the next stage. If it is absolutely necessary to tackle it, it is because of its importance in customs modernisation.

b. The use of high-performance tools by the Chadian customs administration

Globalisation is forcing customs administrations to incorporate certain high-performance tools that are part of modern technology into their modernisation operations. Increasing emphasis is being placed on the scanner system. Generally speaking, a scanner is defined in a documentary memory as "an electronic device that scans a document or any other surface and returns the recorded data in various forms"[40]. From a customs point of view, scanners facilitate customs checks to detect fraud at borders, airports, ports and railway stations. The system can also be used in customs clearance procedures, meaning that scanner-based checks can replace physical checks on goods, just as scanner-based inspections can speed up exit procedures. In some cases, the use of scanners has been combined with risk management methods and techniques using PROFILER[41]software.

In addition, during scanning, the goods remain protected and the processing of operations is greatly accelerated. The scanner plays a primary control role. The aim of deploying a scanner is twofold: on the one hand, speed and, on the other, security in customs operations. As far as speed is concerned, the deployment of The scanner has significantly reduced transit times for containerised goods by replacing intrusive checks with physical checks of goods, which are a source of costs, red tape and multiple hassles for importers. The security aspect is of interest not only to the public authorities[42]but also to economic operators. Seen from these angles, and on the basis of comparative law, it can be said that the scanner has made a positive contribution to customs controls in Cameroon. For example, the installation of a scanner at the port of Douala has not only made it possible to measure the rate of suspicion of a declaration[43], but has also considerably reduced the time taken for goods to pass through, as scanner inspection takes an average of eight minutes compared with several hours for a direct physical visit[44].

As a strategic transit country in the Central African sub-region, Cameroon plays a major role in transit activities. It therefore has an obligation to limit the time taken to process transit files. With this in mind, it has introduced a system for tracking goods by geolocation

(GPS). Goods moving under the transit system are in most cases a source of fraud, as they can easily be manipulated or even changed destination during transport. In order to ensure effective and rapid control, a geolocation system for goods in transit, known as GPS, has been introduced. GPS is a geolocation system for goods in transit through customs, providing real-time information on the cargo. In practice, it consists of applying a beacon to the means of transport which, once connected to the battery, emits a signal. The GPS system is used to track cargo to the point of exit. The setting up of the GPS system has made it possible to control goods in transit through Cameroon and bound for Chad and the Central African Republic thanks to the implementation of its NEXUS++ Cameroon customs GPS application. NEXUS++ Cameroon customs GPS is a Cameroon customs web application dedicated to geolocation tracking of goods declared under the transit procedure and destined for the Republic of Chad and the Central African Republic[45].

The aim of this application is to monitor the actual routing of transit cargo throughout its journey on national territory. The beacons installed on the means of transport are fitted with a chip for satellite tracking. A signal is sent to the server describing the position of the beacon, enabling the tracking team to detect the various movements of the means of transport. Since its introduction, it has led to an unprecedented fall in customs fraud in transit, reduced delays[46]and costs generated by bonds, and simplified customs controls[47].

2. Adopting digital measures to optimise revenue mobilisation

The main objective of modernising the expenditure framework is to enable the State to improve the management of public finances by spending more effectively, i.e. spending less and investing more. The aim is to improve the performance of public spending[48]. Controlling public spending also means spending better, and spending can only be controlled if it is cost-effective. good cost/benefit ratio[49]. Under the influence of new technologies, the Chadian customs administration is undergoing a transformation by introducing the e-GUCE form at its one-stop shops, and is taking full advantage of this to achieve the revenue optimisation and control objectives set by the State.

That said, the digitisation of customs procedures, with a view to raising more revenue, is taking place mainly through the transition from the physical GUCE to the electronic single window[50]. In this regard, the CEMAC legislator has taken the trouble to point out in paragraph (4) of Article 66 of the new CEMAC Customs Code that customs collaborates with national administrations and border control bodies to set up and operate the single window or E-GUCE, using information technology[51].

The question of automating customs formalities[52], which is becoming a topical issue in the sub-region these days, is of interest to countries such as Chad, where the poor performance of customs revenue[53]is still deplored by national authorities and independent analysts. This is why Kebir mahamat ABDOULAYE acknowledged in 2017 that Chadian customs "generates an average of CFAF 300 billion in tax and administrative revenue for the public treasury each year. However, for several decades, Chadian customs had become a sector where tax evasion, the organisation and power of mafia groups (well organised), nepotism, the instability of officials, etc. have become models and have developed well. These phenomena caused hundreds of billions of euros to be lost. FCFA in revenue to the public treasury"([54]). However, the head of the customs office at Hassan Djamouss Airport, Mr Abdoulaye Garimo, stated in an interview that after one month of launching the ASYCUDA WORD system, customs revenue at the airport had doubled thanks to this new system for automating procedures. At the coordination meeting on 31 October 2022, the Director General of Customs in Cameroon, Mr FONGOD Edwin NUVAGA, said that, thanks to automated methods for clearing goods through customs, customs revenues would increase b y 2022. According to the head of the statistics unit, Raphael Hamadjam, Cameroon Customs, in terms of economic performance, mobilised revenue of 897.4 billion CFA francs, i.e. a surplus of 33.5 billion CFA francs, in line with the target set by the State, which was estimated at 863.9 billion CFA francs[55]. This represents an increase of 5.3% on 2021 revenues. For the 2023 financial year, customs revenue is expected to be CFAF 1,004.7 billion[56].

The one-stop shop has been a resounding success and is now widely used throughout the CEMAC customs territory. This marks a real advance by the CEMAC legislator in facilitating customs procedures for the benefit of the customs administration, and even economic operators have found relief thanks to these advances.

B. Economic operators benefit from the replacement of traditional customs clearance methods with automatic ones

International trade operations cost economic operators time and money. Digitalisation has provided them with a A technical instrument to reduce costs and facilitate the process. So there's no escaping digitisation if you want to trade and stay on the trade market in the long term. Computer networks have brought a very positive change of perspective to the customs clearance process, for economic operators too, by making certain formerly compulsory formalities optional for some and unnecessary for others. This simplification is also reflected in the rights (**2**) and obligations (**1**) incumbent on third parties.

1. Priority application of digital measures to facilitate trade

Training, information and support for users and all those involved in the chain is a key task for the one-stop shop (GUCE)[57]. The challenges of digitising customs procedures for import and export operations, as set out in the AFE's recommendations, are the leitmotiv. The Single Window in Chad has viable prospects for the future with "big data" and "blockchain"."Blockchain"[58]. To implement automatic customs clearance methods, the new CEMAC customs legislation requires traders to make detailed declarations, mainly by electronic means[59]. Article 67 of the new Customs Code, publication and availability of information, the conservation of documents and other electronic information, article 78 of the aforementioned code.

In comparison, at the Douala one-stop shop, users are entitled to follow-up support. The Hotline is a 24-hour online service available to users. It receives and resolves incidents relating to the connection, procedures and online files by email and telephone[60]. All port staff are trained in procedures and the use of new technologies. At the GUCE, training and awareness-raising take the form of free training and information sessions for companies and foreign trade users. In addition, users can access all the information they need at the click of a button via various digital tools[61]or on the official one-stop shop website[62]. In terms of facilitating costs, customer-users can pay customs debts using a variety of simple, fast and secure payment methods. In addition to online payment by bank card, other payment methods include online banking (E-banking), mobile phone banking (Mobil-banking), automated teller machines (ATMs) and money transfer agencies (local service points).

Whatever payment method is chosen, the process remains the same: the operator selects the debts he wants to pay and creates a basket; a payment code is automatically assigned to the basket in question; the code is used by the operator to make the payment; once the payment operation has been completed, the operator can use the code to make the payment.A receipt, generated automatically by the system, is sent by email to the debtor's email address. In this regard, Pascal COLIN has stated that "we don't go paperless because it's more secure, but because it's more economical"[63]. Indeed, the main advantage that companies intend to derive from the digitisation of customs procedures for goods is the reduction in costs in a highly competitive environment. The use of a trusted third party is a source of additional costs[64]. It is quite difficult to convince a small African shipper to pay for the of electronic signature. After having spent a lot of money buying a ticket the purchase of the goods in France or China, the transport and the insurance, to spend yet more money on the management of an electronic signature by a trusted third party. He will prefer to send his bill of lading by express courier, which would be less costly.

2. The application of digital measures to secure the flow of information and goods

The digitisation of customs procedures also has the advantage of optimising the flow of information in the chain. This flow presupposes that developers have programmed the entire process. In today's fast-paced business environment, optimising the flow of information in the chain is the key to success. Sending a bill of lading from the port of Marseille to Chad by post will take around two to three weeks to be delivered to the addressee by post, and around one to two days by express specialists such as FEDEX and DHL[65]. However, in a digitised environment, circulation and transmission are instantaneous.

This is to the advantage of economic operators. They have all the time they need to anticipate customs procedures while waiting for the ship to arrive. When the ship docks, its DAC will validate the declaration online and transmit it to customs via the same channel. Organising customs clearance in this way avoids the additional costs (parking, demurrage) associated with delays in transmitting physical documents. In practical terms, digitising customs procedures helps to facilitate transport for suppliers, shippers and consignees.

For the carrier, digitisation means that manifest bundles can be transmitted online to all the authorities responsible for transport in just one click, particularly customs. For the shipper, thanks to digitisation "For the shipper, thanks to dematerialisation, the booking, checking, issuing and transmission of bills of lading can now be done online, avoiding the need for multiple trips to the office. Despite the considerable progress made by Chadian customs in computerising the customs clearance process, a number of difficulties have been encountered in implementing these measures, making their effectiveness hypothetical.

II. PERFORMANCE HAMPERED BY DIFFICULTIES IN APPLYING AUTOMATIC CUSTOMS CLEARANCE PROCEDURES

The Internet revolution is overturning ways of thinking, legal and administrative traditions, and the rules of competition. It is creating a situation of uncertainty with largely unpredictable developments, calling into question the State's usual intellectual framework and methods[66]. It is on this basis that it can be deduced that digitised customs procedures may be weakened by any attacks on the confidentiality, integrity and availability of computer systems and the data stored, processed or transmitted by these systems[67]. In 1972, Dean Jean CARBONNIER stated that "changes in morals and technology give rise to new forms of delinquency"[68]. In the same vein, Samuel Tepi describes these as "new loopholes"[69]. These difficulties in implementing digital customs procedures in Chad affect every link in the customs chain. The customs administration has not been spared. That said, the optimisation of the performance of the logistics chain brought about by the digitisation of customs procedures in Chad is challenged by a number of disadvantages associated with access to digital technology (**A**) and resistance to it (B). of the customs administration to adapt to the modern or digital process of clearing goods through customs (**B**).

A. The weakening of modern customs procedures linked to the right of access to the Internet

One of the most formidable problems in Chad, and indeed in most CEMAC Member States, affecting the automation of customs procedures is undoubtedly that of offences[70]relating to unauthorised access to and maintenance of a computer system (**1**). Secondly, data sabotage and computer sabotage (**2**).

1. Failures linked to the digital divide

The failures linked to Internet access and electrical energy will be the subject of this sub-section.

Permanent high-speed Internet access remains a major challenge for businesses and customs administrations. Internet access is provided by institutional players, Internet service and access providers, and economic interest groups under the supervision of the national telecommunications regulatory authorities. According to some observers, the high cost of Internet access is due to the very limited capacity of international network connections (cable and satellite).

This is particularly true in landlocked countries such as Chad. Chad is not connected to the countries that have access to it, and is therefore limited to low-capacity and very expensive satellite connections. Another reason given for this is the limited number of copper lines and the dubious quality of the existing ones for broadband access. To date, Chad, like the majority of CEMAC member states, is not yet in a position to invest in a satellite, given the cost of the operation. It is aware of the need for a reliable and secure telecommunications network to digitise data in the country. However, the regional Central Africa Backbone[71]programme supported by the World Bank, if completed, could significantly reduce the digital divide and put an end to the instability of the Internet network in Chad. Until this happens, however, customs procedures are still not being digitised.

Inadequate equipment and unequal access to the network mean that information cannot be circulated in real time[72]. An analysis of the Internet connection value chain in Chad reveals a number of shortcomings in investment in basic infrastructure[73]. The monopoly of incumbent operators on existing infrastructure is well known. Hence the high cost of providing a connection. The malfunctioning of Chad's Internet networks is not conducive to the digitisation of customs procedures. The fibre optic network used extensively in Chad, alongside satellites, is experiencing instability due to technical problems and acts of vandalism by local people[74].That said, it is up to the Société Tchadienne des Télécommunications (SOTEL), created by Law No. 009/PR/98 with the task of providing public goods and services in the area of mobile and fixed telephony, to ensure interconnection, access and infrastructure sharing[75]with all other operators in the country, such as Airtel and Tigo. SOTEL's interconnection offer includes value-added services[76]such as termination of international voice traffic[77]on the SOTEL network, resale of traffic[78], audiotex service and internet service. Service and connection offers such as satellite services, SAT3[80]WACS and NCSCS fibre optic submarine cable[79]links, co-location[81]offers and infrastructure sharing, including the hosting of terminal equipment, masts, etc. In order to clear themselves of the Internet outages and the poor connection that the country is experiencing, mobile telephone operators invoke above all the increase in taxes[82];In fact, the tax revenues collected from the mobile telephony sector fall into two categories: revenues from taxes borne directly by these operators and revenues from taxes borne by end consumers but collected by the operators on behalf of the Treasury. Regardless of the contributor, these levies have an impact on the following It also has a negative impact on mobile operators' turnover, by adversely affecting the consumption of mobile services. This confirms the idea that reducing the tax burden on mobile telephony could lead to a reduction in the cost of services and, consequently, an increase in their consumption. This would lead to an increase in turnover, which in turn would have an impact on the pace of investment[83]. The taxation of Internet turnover (in terms of excise duty) is also not in line with Directive N°07/11- UEAC-028-CM- 22 of 19 December 2011 revising the CEMAC Directive on the harmonisation of the laws of Member States relating to Value Added Tax (VAT) and Excise Duty (ED). Annex 1 of this Directive expressly exempts fixed, wire and internet communications[84]. Taxation of internet revenues is partly responsible for the higher cost of internet connections in Chad compared with other countries in the sub-region. Another cause of network instability is the fact that Chad does not have enough Internet Exchange Points (IXPs). Data transits through servers sometimes located a thousand miles from the continent. To deal with instability and insufficient bandwidth, "governments can adopt policies to support new technologies, new business models and investment. Appropriate policies will then encourage the private sector to deploy the necessary infrastructure and explore new technologies and applications that will fuel demand"[85]. The issue of integration is therefore insidiously back on the table to encourage the CEMAC countries to work together to find common solutions for continuous high-speed Internet access in an optimised network. "Let's be realistic: no single player will be able to achieve the 2030 objective and support the 100 billion dollars of investment required. All stakeholders must agree and work together to ensure that all Africans have access to an affordable internet connection"[86]. The World Bank, the African Union and the regional economic communities are therefore calling on African governments and their public investment bodies, as well as all stakeholders in the development of infrastructure and equipment. It's a question of tackling the Internet deficit, but also the energy deficit.

As far as Chad's energy shortfall is concerned, we can say that despite an enormous potential in solar and renewable energies, the country has major energy deficits. For the latter, untimely power cuts are frequent, and even more so in the dry season. The hydroelectric dams are crumbling under the weight of age and in need of renovation. The maintenance of facilities that have become obsolete in the face of strong demand must be accompanied by the acquisition of modern equipment. To put it plainly, the energy deficit is a major blow to Chad's economic development, and is reflected in the untimely and recurrent power cuts known as "load shedding". These power cuts punctuate the daily life of businesses and limit the digitisation of customs procedures in Chad. A common electrification policy could reduce the scale of this scourge and the prerogatives arising from controls.

2. Shortcomings in customs control prerogatives

The limits to customs prerogatives are constituted by the need to respect the confidentiality of private data (**a**) and the preservation of individual liberties (**b**).

a. Failure to respect the confidentiality of private data

It is to be feared that the exercise of the control prerogatives of the public authorities, which are legally devolved to them, may lead to infringements of the privacy of ordinary economic operators. It is easy for the public authorities or any other institution to invoke the pretext of seeking information to gain access to data which are the private property of economic operators[87]. Hence the need to regulate access to this information and restrict it to just what is necessary to identify and locate the operator. In this spirit, the virtual world of the Internet, by breaking with traditional rationales, casts in a different light the delicate problem of the balance between the need for control and that intimate dimension of man which is the very essence of his humanity. Striking the right balance between the rights of the individual and the need for control to ensure collective security is only achieved in the physical world at the cost of multiple confrontations and historical developments. Moreover, this necessary balance between freedom and security is never intangible. The level of balance is always contingent and varies according to the political, economic and social context. This explains why, in these times of heightened security concerns, a series of measures are being taken around the world, with the major consequence of undermining individual rights. The Internet, the seat of human interaction par excellence, is no exception to this permanent struggle between two highly contradictory imperatives, which any political society must overcome or risk disappearing. It is therefore necessary for a climate of consultation to be established between the community of Internet users on the one hand, and the national public authorities and international institutions on the other, so that fair enough operating rules can be established that can preserve intangible and inalienable human rights, which strongly include security[88].

b. Failure to preserve individual freedoms

The individual freedoms of economic operators can be violated in two ways: on the one hand, by the mechanism of "hacking" into their accounts, and on the other hand, by the customs administration, which by virtue of its control prerogatives does not respect the balance.

The most high-profile aspect of attacks using new technologies at the moment is the unauthorised intrusion into computer systems or "hacking". Hacking is now one of the most popular activities in the dematerialised world of the global network. This practice of the "Internet underground"[89]is a game for some, a provocation for others, and a way of making one's demands known for the third. Hacking is currently a significant part of online activity. It can be carried out by the merely curious, but also by companies or mafias for the purposes of espionage and industrial or political sabotage. The current dimension of this "hacking" activity is the result in particular of the development of computer networks and the entry of companies onto the Internet through services and information provided to customers or e-commerce offers, which often give hackers access to systems that they can use to commit crimes. the company's IT systems. However, a major issue remains to be clarified[90]. It relates to the determination of this notion of illicit access. When can access to a computer system be qualified as illicit?On the other hand, the exercise of the right of communication or the right of access must not be used as a pretext to infringe the privacy or personal freedoms of individuals. Indeed, a great deal of information relating to the intimate lives of individuals is, by necessity, stored on the Net. Consequently, no service should be allowed unlimited and uncontrolled access to this data. From this point of view, strict control by the judiciary, the guarantor of individual freedoms, is necessary to prevent any abuse. Given the potential risks that penetration by a third party, even the customs authorities, may present for individual freedoms, but also for the privacy of individuals, prior to any introduction into an internal network giving access to the Internet, but from the installations of an operator or service provider, authorisation must be given by the liberties and detention judge, as is the case in the current procedure for the right of visit in cases of flagrante delicto[91]. This order should be subject only to an appeal to the Supreme Court, but above all, the appeal should not have suspensive effect. Information circulates in real time on the global network and, what is more, it is easy for all traces of a transaction to disappear in a short space of time. Hence the need for the customs service to act quickly and efficiently to find the necessary and relevant information. In truth, giving suspensive effect to the appeal against the order of the liberty and custody judge does not help to make the customs service's action effective. This is because it allows the operator, who does not want certain information to be collected by the customs service, to erase all traces of the compromising information in a very short space of time. Again in the spirit of preserving individual freedoms and protecting privacy, officers must inform the public prosecutor before entering the premises of an operator or service provider, in the exercise of their right to visit or communicate via the Internet. The public prosecutor must be able to be notified by any means, given the need for rapidity, but also, when he considers that the exercise of these customs prerogatives is unjustified, he must oppose any access to the network. Lastly, a record of the operations must be drawn up and sent to the customs authorities within a reasonable time, and a copy of the record must be sent to the person concerned.

B. The Chadian customs administration's resistance to modern digital mechanisms

These shortcomings are reflected in customs officers' resistance to change (**1**), which sometimes poorly conceals the incompetence of human resources (**2**).

1. Customs officers' resistance to modern mechanisms for clearing goods through customs

Resistance to digital technology is noticeable in the administrations in charge of managing customs affairs. managing customs affairs. This is reflected in a high level of resistance to to change. Faced with the new challenges posed by the digitisation of goods clearance procedures, customs administrations are having to change radically. This requires total change, which means sacrificing the advantages that everyone has created in a material environment marked by bureaucracy and bribes. Administrative reluctance in Chad is a daily reality for customs officers. Chad's public and semi-public sector in general, and the customs and the customs administration in particular, has often painted a bleak picture of an administration that has been a breeding ground for inertia, bureaucracy, corruption, profiteering, extortion and document fraud. All of which have contributed to an erosion of professionalism and a decline in ethics among public officials. Governments are struggling to paint this bleak picture, despite the various catharsis initiatives undertaken by public authorities to dismantle the barriers between users and public officials. While everyone agrees that digitisation has many advantages, it has to be said that administrative reluctance is a major limit to the computerisation of documents passing through public officials. Yet "the influence of dematerialisation on the environment, society and people is undeniable"[92]. It makes everyday life easier for citizens by simplifying administrative procedures, and for businesses by streamlining processes. It reduces costs and gives everyone access to information. It is creating new ways of working remotely and reducing the need to travel. One day, it will replace the vast quantities of paper consumed around the world, with greater respect for the environment as a result. The impact of dematerialisation on the economy, the environment and society is therefore undeniable. Such a vision does not seem to be shared by the customs administration in Chad, which is noticeably reluctant to implement the digitalisation of customs procedures in practice. Clearly, resistance to change is seen first and foremost in the customs administration, and then extends to other administrations involved in clearing goods through customs, such as the health, environment, autonomous port, livestock, fisheries and animal industries, trade, gendarmerie and police services. These administrations remain very attached to physical documents and would have no interest in seeing the digitisation of customs procedures promoted to the highest level by the Heads of State prosper[93]. The reason for this resistance to change is that digitising customs procedures is an undeniable tool in the fight against the corruption that is undermining the country's economy. In the field, in a port such as Douala, it is not uncommon for the customs authorities to force users to go to customs to validate their customs file, even though the file has already been validated by customs on the CAMSIS[94]platform, which contains all the information relating to the goods. What's more, it is not out of the question for customs to require users to present original commercial documents, even for goods in transit.

2. Inadequate human resources skills in the use of new technologies

The mastery of digital tools by producers and users is inadequate and poses a problem of human resources training. The absence or inadequacy of training for competent human resources in the service of digitising customs procedures poses a serious problem. As a result, stakeholders are finding that digitisation is costing them time and money. Indeed, the United Nations Economic Commission for Africa has pointed out that "the most crucial challenges facing institutions involved in skills development include difficulties in recruiting trainers and teachers, lack of scholarships to support students, financial resources to manage new programmes and resistance to change"[95]. The shortage of human resources is much more acute in developing countries, where there is a shortage of teachers and trainers. people trained in new technologies are rare, it remains a global problem. Just look at the frenzy of headhunters on the web looking for IT profiles[96].

CONCLUSION

Ultimately, there is no doubt that the digitisation of customs procedures is helping to facilitate the process of clearing goods through customs, by simplifying procedures and making information flows more secure. This transformation contributes to sustainable economic development and the optimisation of lead times and revenues in the logistics chain. However, the lack of training for customs officers and economic operators does little to encourage the emergence and easy implementation of this laudable initiative in Chad. It should also be noted that, specifically, the lack of modern logistical infrastructure to support the digitisation of the customs clearance process also remains a handicap. So, in order to reap these benefits in the long term, the Chadian customs administration has a fundamental role to play. This is to adopt and implement genuine policies for digitising procedures and their economy. The example of developed countries can be followed, while respecting the realities of the Chadian context, in order to create a more fluid market. This can be done with the support of facilitation bodies such as Guichets uniques (one-stop shops) and national trade facilitation committees to improve the performance of the customs administration.

BIBLIOGRAPHICAL REFERENCES

• **ADOU (J.-M.),** Modernisation du circuit de la dépense publique en Côte d'Ivoire et efficacité de la dépense, Master's thesis in public administration, 2005.

• **AYESSA (A.),** Eléments de droit douanier, des procédures et techniques douanières dans les Etats membres de la CEMAC, Paris, Connaissance et savoirs, 2010.

• **BELOTTI (J.),** Transport international des marchandises, 5ᵉed. Magnard-Vuibert, January 2015.

• **BERR (C.) et TREMEAU (H.),** Le droit douanier communautaire et national, 7ᵉéd, Paris, Economica, 2006.

• **BILANGNA (S.),** La réforme des douanes camerounaises: entre les contraintes locales et internationales, Afrique contemporaine, 2009/2 (No. 230).

• **CARBONNIER (J.),** "Sociologie juridique", published by A. Colin, 1972, édition PUF, coll Thémis, Paris, 1978, Refondue coll. Quadrige 1994 et 2004.

• **CHEVALLIER (J.),** "La politique française de modernisation administrative", in l'Etat de droit, Mélange en l'honneur de **BRAIBANT (G.**), Dalloz, Paris, 1996.

• **COLIN (P.),** "Dématérialisation en entreprise, de quoi les français ont-ils peur? Le cas des fiches de paie numériques", Finyear, 2016.

• **DEUTSCH (J-C.) and VULLIERME (M.),** L'évolution des techniques. In Flux, 2003.

• **GUELLEC (D.)**, Économie de l'innovation, Paris, édition de la découverte, 2017.

• **LANNEAU (R.),** "qu'entend-on par la maitrise des dépenses publiques?", RGFP,n° 11, 2013.

• **LIBOM LI LIKENG (M.),** " Performance et discipline budgétaire : Les leviers de la performance douanière, exposé du DGD à la conférence du MINFI les 2212 ", in revue des douanes camerounaises n° 29 avril, 2014.

• **MAFO TSHINDA (C.),** "Les mesures de facilitation des échanges dans le cadre des contrôles douaniers au Cameroun", IMJST, Vol. 5, 2020.

• **MINE OKON (A-B.), DJEUWO (M.) et PAGOU (L.),** " Performance de la chaine portuaire et flux commerciaux : le cas du port de Douala ", Rapport de performance, 2021.

• **MONTAGNAT-RENTIER (G.), & PARENT (G.),** "Réforme et modernisation des douanes en Afrique subsaharienne francophone 1995-2010", Revue d'économie du développement, 2012.

- **NYAMA (J-M.),** Droit douanier de la CEMAC, Cerfod, 2000.
- **PEKASSA NDAM (G.),** "Les transformations de l'administration fiscale camerounaise". **ONDOA (M.)** (ed.) L'administration publique camerounaise à l'heure des réformes, Paris, L'Harmattan, 2010.
- **TEPI (S.),** La cybercriminalité au Cameroun, Enjeux d'une législation en quête d'efficacité, Paris, l'Harmattan, 2020.

TABLE OF CONTENTS

Kolibri 360 GmbH
Ferdinand-Jühlke-Straße 7
99095 Erfurt, Deutschland
produktsicherheit@kolibri360.de

Druck:
CPI Druckdienstleistungen GmbH
im Auftrag der
Kolibri 360 GmbH
Ferdinand-Jühlke-Str. 7
99095 Erfurt